Building Great Boards

*Insights for startups and small business -
From a master entrepreneur and friends*

Third Edition with Expanded and New Material

Dave Berkus

With Girard Miller and Maryann Bryla

Published by David Berkus DBA The Berkus Press

For corrections, company/title updates, comments, or any other inquiries, please email DBerkus@berkus.com

Third printing 2023
10 9 8 7 6 5 4 3

ISBN 978-1-105-04074-0

Copyright © 2014-2023 by David W. Berkus. All rights reserved. Printed in the United States of America. No part of this publication may be reproduced or distributed in any form or by any means, or stored in a database or retrieval system, except as permitted under Sections 107 or 108 of the U.S. Copyright Act, without prior written permission of the publisher. This book is printed on acid-free paper.

Material in this book is for educational purposes only. This book is sold with the understanding that neither the author nor the publisher is engaged in rendering legal, accounting, investment, or any other professional service. Neither the publisher nor the author assumes any liability for any errors or omissions, or for how this book or its contents are used or interpreted, or for any consequences resulting directly or indirectly from the use of this book. For legal advice or any other, please consult your personal lawyer or the appropriate professional.

Some of the content within this book has been previously published within the books, BASIC BERKONOMICS, BERKONOMICS, and ADVANCED BERKONOMICS. Individual insights from this book are published periodically in Dave's emails and blog, www.berkonomics.com.

Groups may order copies of the book at a group discount by contacting Dave Berkus at 626-355-5375, or at dberkus@berkus.com .

Throughout this book, the Cambria type font was used for headlines, and text was set using the Calibri font.

The views expressed by the individuals in this book do not necessarily reflect the views shared by the companies they are employed by (or the companies mentioned in) this book. The employment status and affiliations of the author with the companies referenced are subject to change.

Contents

INTRODUCTION 6

Additional contributors to this book: 7

Back to basics: Boards of directors protect and help to grow the enterprise. 9

Outside directors are a price of investment 11

Prospective members: Are you prepared to assume a board seat? 14

Early-stage boards work for stock options not cash. 16

What to expect in board member commitment. 17

Consider the evolution of a board from startup to exit. 18

You'll learn as you teach when on a great board. 19

Find an outside confidant, a CEO coach. 21

How would you like a great advisory board? 21

An experienced coach has seen your movie before. 23

Don't forget those informal "grab a lunch" advisors. 26

Great relationships are among your most valuable assets. 27

Boards of directors protect the corporation first. 28

Strategy and stewardship go hand in hand. 30

How bold or confrontational should a board member be? 32

The need for a board grows with complexity. 34

Did the company incorporate in the right state? 36

Fight for balance on your board. 38

Board members should be elected annually. 39

Good board members are as valuable as good executives. 40

To you directors: Noses in, fingers out. 41

How about your board meetings? Schedules and attendance matter. 42

Agendas frame the key discussions. Minutes foster accountability. 44

Feed your board with constant care and attention. 46

How about communication and obligations to Investors? 47

D&O insurance is a "cost of respect" for board members. 48

Here's a rule that can "save" a board! 49

Be sure the Board and CEO are in alignment. 50

Product-market fit: An important board subject for growth or survival 53

Be a detective: Watch for early warning signs and signals. 54

Any advice can be worthless, or worse. 56

Guard the Gold. 58

Do you always follow the advice of your board? 59

A good board deals with what and why, not how. 60

What if the CEO is the problem? 61

One board function: Assessing, shaping, and coaching the management team 62

What to do with a dysfunctional board. 64

Use your board's "golden contacts." 66

Separate the chairmanship from the CEO position. 67

No negative surprises! Be first to warn of shortfalls............ 70

Following up: Make your surprises positive........................... 72

What's in it for me? Think like your stakeholders................. 73

This way to the exit: thinking strategically........................... 74

About the author… ***77***

Other books by Dave Berkus available directly from *www.berkus.com* or from your favorite bookseller or online store: 79

INTRODUCTION

This book is one in a series of eight short, easy to read books that guide an entrepreneur through the stages of creation, management, growth, and ultimately sale of a small business enterprise. And this is the third edition of this book, packed with new materials from co-authors that extend the reach and value of the first edition, published in 2011 and the second edition from 2017.

Each section is an insight into another facet of starting a business that is not taught in business school or available in business texts, but rather the result of over fifty years of entrepreneurial experience with my own entrepreneurial companies and serving as investor, coach, mentor and board member for over forty entrepreneurial startups over the years.

Originally published as portions of three books, BASIC BERKONOMICS, BERKONOMCS, and ADVANCED BERKONOMICS, comments from entrepreneurs and professional managers after reading those books led to suggestions that I create separate mini books for each stage of the business, to appeal to the interests of those at that stage of development, ready to absorb and implement insights that apply directly to the current stage of their business. Make them inexpensive and available as eBooks, they suggested, so that entire teams of managers could use the book as a planning tool and discussion prompt for the team in meetings.

And so, this series of Small Business Success Books was born to address an opportunity. You can pick up this book and immediately relate to the insights, issues, opportunities, and exercises in this book right at the earliest stages of creating your business, or in this case perhaps becoming a member of a model board of directors or advisors. This is not a replacement for "how to" books, courses, and consultants. It is a deeper opportunity to evaluate, plan, and execute strategies for growth based upon these insights that augment and amplify the usual "how to" materials available to entrepreneurs.

In this book, I'll tell personal stories from my fifty-plus years of entrepreneurial experience. But every one of us has a story to add to this mix, one of passionate entrepreneurism, sometimes inside an existing larger corporation, sometimes alone on a kitchen table, or back-room desk. And it is a sure thing that many of us will have cogent, insightful additions to this caldron, culled from their own experiences. There's a place for these in the blog, www.berkonomics.com, and I welcome any and all for others to read and learn.

Dave Berkus

Arcadia, California

P.S. This is the sixteenth publication from *The Berkus Press*. I am fortunate to have expert help this time from some very smart friends in the business, each of whom has volunteered to contribute insights for this book, directly from their personal experience of working as an entrepreneur or with entrepreneurs. Here's a special thanks to these friends, whose contributions are definitely for your benefit. Whenever one of these excellent insights appears in this book, the name of that contributor will appear below its headline. And as always, if no attribution appears for an insight, I'm its author - and to be blamed for any and all errors in judgment and accuracy.

Additional contributors to this book:

__Girard Miller__ is a seasoned investor and former mutual fund executive, with governance experience across the corporate, governmental, and nonprofit sectors. A previous White House adviser retired chartered financial analyst and two-time CEO with Sarbanes-Oxley reporting responsibilities, his focus nowadays is tending to his own diversified portfolio and writing a biweekly column for Governing Finance. He is an active member of the Tech Coast Angels Orange County chapter.

Maryann Bryla is a successful serial entrepreneur, CEO of her own capital advisory firm. She has decades of experience as a Board Director of various global corporations. She is a former CFO of a large, diversified media, cable and technology company where she successfully negotiated and closed over $8.5 Billion in M&A transactions. Maryann began her finance career on Wall Street, has raised over $3.5 Billion in the public capital markets and is an active investor in many early-stage companies through her own investment funds.

William De Temple is a seasoned executive with experience in turn-around and start-up ventures. As CEO of Maximize Management, Inc., he oversees work with turn-around and growth company clients nationwide. William is also founder of The Enterprise Training Academy.

Building Great Boards

A great CEO is not afraid to listen to and take advice from experienced players in business and the industry. With the ease of today's communication in its many frictionless forms over the Internet, I find myself giving and getting advice about specific problems without the usual social time spent in personal communication. You've got to know and be comfortable with the person on the opposite end of the keyboard or Zoom video, but it works.

In fact, great CEO's invite help and welcome criticism and guidance. In this stage of a business's development, we'll explore the insights relating to finding, nurturing, compensating and acting upon advice from coaches, board members and advisors.

Back to basics: **Boards of directors protect and help to grow the enterprise.**

No matter what your size, if you intend to grow your business into more than just a lifestyle workplace, you should create a board of directors. If you take money from knowledgeable investors, you will be required to create a board as a part of the investment process.

Boards perform two important types of tasks. They protect the company by overseeing the expenditure of company money for expansion, acquisitions, purchases of large assets, hiring of senior management and more. A board is usually composed of a mixture of the senior executives or the CEO, at least one representative of the investors, and at least one industry expert from outside the company. The usual size of an early-stage board is five, but legally the number in most states is equal to the number of shareholders up to a maximum of three board members required by law. With three or more shareholders, you must have a three-person board of directors in most states. The average board for a company taking outside investment money is five. Beyond seven members, a board is often too cumbersome to be of the most effective value to the CEO.

Each board member is legally tasked with two duties: the duty of care, and the duty of loyalty: care for the living entity that is the corporation itself, and loyalty not to the board member's constituency, but to the corporation itself. Sometimes, these duties conflict with the best interests of the board member personally or his or her co-investors. This could happen when a board votes to take in new money at terms that would be unfavorable to the class of investor represented by the board member. It could happen if some early investors and board members want to sell the company at a price below the objective of the later board member, where the relative returns are excellent for the early investors and marginal for the later ones.

There is no legally mandated requirement that members of the board help a corporation to grow. But it is certainly the goal of the investors, the CEO and even the board members individually, when assuming the position of board member. Often, a board meeting is entirely devoted to issues of growth, with members chiming in to help the CEO with marketing issues or customer acquisition.

It is important to make time for the required duties at board meetings. Approving the budget and watching over it during the year and approving any actions that would dilute ownership including stock option grants, are two examples. Much less understood are issues that address the management of risk, such as review of corporate insurance policies, adherence to OSHA safety regulations, and oversight of the terms of real estate and large equipment leases that could affect a company's ability to maneuver in times of crisis or extreme growth.

Many entrepreneurs would rather not have to answer to a board, and resist creating an entity that could have the power to check management actions, and even to fire the CEO in extreme cases. Yet, the establishment of a proactive board is the first step toward professionalizing the company and its management. Properly handled by the CEO with adequate time allocation for individual and group board member updates, the proper use of the board will help control risk and provide resources to management that will pay back in better overall management of the company and more efficient use of its resources. More importantly, no entrepreneur or CEO can do it all alone, especially in a rapid growth scenario. Too many things can go wrong, many of which are things that one or more board members have already dealt with in their business lives.

Take the establishment and nurture of a board of directors seriously. It is much more than a legal requirement to be resolved. It is the creation of a vital part of the organization, one that could be of great help in both the protection and growth of the enterprise. Great boards create value for shareholders while protecting them at the same time.

Outside directors are a price of investment.

Once a company founder has tapped the funds available from his or her resources and from friends and family, if the company needs more cash for growth, the most obvious next step is to look for money from angel investors and venture capitalists, typically in the $300,000 TO $3,000,000 range. This money comes with restrictions a founder may not expect, including restrictions upon the sale of founder stock, clauses that require the investor be allowed to sell an equal proportion of stock upon any other person's sale of stock, anti-dilution provisions that protect the investor from a subsequent offer of stock at a lower price, and much more. Almost always, professional investors, including angel groups and venture capitalists, also require at least one seat on the corporate board. The investor organization is granted the seat as long as the investment remains, and the documents often name the first representative assigned by the investor group to the position.

In subsequent insights, we will explore the legal and ethical responsibilities of board members. But the intent of these "forced" placements of a representative on the board is obviously to watch over the company's use of invested funds and to help grow the company in value. The combination of restrictive covenants in the investor documents and the new dynamic of board members with an agenda make for a change in the culture of the corporation, certainly one for the CEO.

However, outside professional investor board members can be a very good asset to the corporation with the skills, experience and broad relationships many bring to the boardroom table.

Look before you leap!

By Gerard Miller

In many ways, board service is like marriage. It's a long-term commitment for better or worse. With half of most startups failing ultimately, the downside risks should not be overlooked. Quickie marriages, elopements and shotgun marriages usually end sadly. The same is true for directors who join a board without "looking under the hood."

A candid discussion between a prospective director and the CEO (and other founders, where relevant) may include important topics such as:

- How many directors are authorized and how many are now serving? What's their relationship to the CEO/founders? How many independent investors are now on the board, and why?
- What's the plan, if any, for adding new directors in the future?
- What are the skill-sets, expertise and networks that the board most needs now? What weak spots do the CEO and founders self-identify in themselves? Their board? Their team?
- How much interaction with directors during meetings and between meetings does the CEO expect, prefer, and welcome? Does the CEO provide tools to the board for an annual performance assessment and candid discussions of areas for performance improvement?
- Is there an "alpha" director who commonly leads the board with the expectation of supporting votes? If so, how does that work? Are issues decided before meetings begin?
- How does the board deal with dissent? Challenges? Devil's advocates? How does the CEO react and interact with differing opinions, suggestions and strategies?
- How does the management team interact with the board? Who's weakest? Who's strong?
- How often are regular meetings scheduled? When are agendas and advance readings sent?
- Who's the attorney, auditor, and board secretary?
- What financial, personnel and legal issues and problems will I be walking into?
- Does the CEO regularly update the board on budgets, staffing, KPIs, cash burn/runway?
- What has been the most contentious issue the board has faced in the past year?
- What's now keeping the CEO awake at night? Who's helping to address that concern?

We don't intend to address all these questions in this short book. But this does provide a great checklist for you in a discussion with the founder(s) or CEO before accepting a seat on the board.

Prospective members: Are you prepared to assume a board seat?
By Gerard Miller

Before accepting a board seat, as a prospective director, you should establish a basic understanding of the company's legal form and governance structure.

So, for a start, here are basic questions to ask: Where is the company incorporated and domiciled as a legal entity? Who holds the original copies of the articles of incorporation and bylaws, and what other central corporate documents now exist?

Look over the bylaws and find how many directors are authorized and required in the corporate documents. Who are the company's officers, by title and by name? Be aware that some states such as California require a minimum number of directors (in California's case, one per shareholder up to a maximum of three, beyond which the State does not care.)

And here's a very important one we will cover again in this book: Do the bylaws provide blanket or limited indemnification for directors? If so, what kinds of actions could disqualify a director from indemnification? Which states will be relevant due to sales activities, offices, or resident employees for tax purposes? What do the bylaws say about the frequency of meetings of the board, quorum and voting procedures, and obligations of the individual directors? What is the prescribed process for amendments of corporate documents?

Don't hesitate to ask for copies of the key documents. Consider this "thrilling reading," as the things you will learn are not only important but may make you the go-to expert in such matters in board meetings.

If possible, you should speak with corporate counsel, to understand why the articles of incorporation were established in the company's legal state of domicile. Ask whether any state laws impose specific requirements on the composition and size of the board of directors (see example state above).

This next one gets a bit dicey when the CEO is a founder: Does the company have an employment agreement with the CEO? Do any other managers have employment agreements? Have individual employees signed agreements certifying that intellectual property they develop on the job stating clearly that this belongs to the company? How about a confidentiality agreement signed by each employee? In that vein, how is intellectual property such as patents registered and owned?

Are there any loans or other corporate legal obligations that encumber assets or revenues of the company that impact decisions to be made by the board? Any legal judgments that restrict the board's business decision-making processes and authority?

Once each year, the directors should schedule a formal board meeting agenda item for a review of legal matters including the corporate documents, litigation, tax considerations and key contracts. We label this "risk management." The questions in that session can be expanded to include insurance policies, safety issues and disaster plans.

That's a lot. You could become the guide for the board, bringing up these issues for examination – issues which may never have been considered. Let's label these "operational issues." Later in this book, we will consider "generative questions" such as what, why, when, and how. And of course, we'll consider financial questions, which rarely need coaching but are most important, especially to young companies and inexperienced management.

Early-stage boards work for stock options not cash.

Give one percent equity to each outside board member vesting over four years of service.

Many early-stage CEOs and board members have asked for some guidance regarding pay and time commitments for board members. Here is my best advice, based upon many boards and many years. Pay early-stage board members of companies that are not lifestyle businesses one percent of the fully diluted equity in the form of an option that vests over four years of service. The option price should be set by appraisal under IRS rule 409a, and certainly should be low enough to recognize that common stock options are not worth as much as preferred stock, given the many preferences of the latter. Further, the option should contain a special clause that accelerates vesting to 100% upon a change of control in the corporation, which aligns the board member with the best interests of the corporation itself. Otherwise, you might picture an event in which the sale of a company to be consummated a few months before full vesting could cause a board member to find ways to vote for delays or even against a sale of the company, awaiting full vesting of his or her options.

For lifestyle companies or later stage companies, board members should be paid on a per-meeting basis in cash. Typically, this payment amounts to $1,000 per meeting of the board, adjusted upward for public corporations to $3,000 per meeting on average, with special pay for committee chairs and special meetings. These payments recognize that board members are not working for equity but for the equivalent of consulting fees plus the attendant risks of board membership.

Venture investors with investments from their funds are not typically ever offered pay for board service, which is expected as part of the investment. Inside board members, CEO and any other paid employees are not paid for board service in either stock options or cash.

Expenses for travel are often reimbursed by the corporation. VC board members sometimes request this, other times do not. It should not be offered to the VC members unless requested.

The next insight will cover what should be expected of a board member in the way of time allocated to the company.

What to expect in board member commitment.

Expect a board member to give a meeting a month, emails and phone calls between. Urgent issues require more of all.

Board members are usually busy people, often running other companies or serving on multiple boards. Early-stage boards usually meet once a month for two to four hours, enough to ruin the rest of the day for those who travel even short distances. In addition, most board members freely receive phone calls and emails from the CEO during the month, all considered part of the service.

There are times when board members are called upon to give extraordinary time to the corporation, such as interviewing candidates, strategic planning, recovery from a cash flow crisis or other urgent issues. Most often these are freely given by board members.

The line is crossed when a CEO asks a member of the board to consult to the company, spending considerable time with other employees regarding issues that might be handled by others than from a board. Depending upon the board member, it is appropriate to offer a consulting fee for this time spent above the call of board duty. Any such informal contracting of service should always be preceded with an agreement between the CEO and board member as to the amount to charge and estimate of time to be spent before further agreement is necessary.

Consider the evolution of a board from startup to exit.
By Gerard Miller

Many startup companies begin their governance journeys with very small boards, often controlled entirely or overwhelmingly by the founders. By the time an angel investor has joined a board, it may already have expanded from its original size. It is usually about founder control early on. Sometimes the founders and top executives maintain voting control of the board and are resistant to expanding the board unless they can hand-pick the new directors. That could be a yellow flag which deserves a board level discussion. We've already covered the ideal size and mix of a board in earlier insights.

It's all about balance, as you will learn. An ideal governance board includes management, founders, key investor representatives, and industry experts, who all bring value to the enterprise. Not all these need to be voting directors. Remember our insights about advisory boards earlier. And add that you can use some of these advisors as "board observers," attending board meetings without vote, and among those who must leave whenever the chairman asks for an executive session of the board.

One of the most important functions that an experienced investor acting as director is to promote a "family discussion" of the skill sets available to the CEO through the board, its observers, and the company's advisors. The goal should be a broad base of relevant technical and operational expertise, industry connections, marketing insights, and financial and investment expertise, which can be available to the management team and the governing board. Careful: we are not addressing the size of the board here as before, but rather the reach of the board to have resources in these areas.

Half of all early-stage companies ultimately fail or require dramatic pivots to survive. So, the board should eventually be populated with enough independent directors to persuade an underperforming or functionally deficient CEO to step down, step aside or sell to new owners to salvage the company or at least preserve some equity value. Likewise, many startups employ managers who were hand-picked by the original CEO. Their shortcomings may be obvious to independent directors but not to the CEO. This observation and any resulting recommendations require candor, diplomacy, and persuasion skills in a board executive session. Independent directors can provide peripheral vision to the CEO even when the message is difficult.

And here's one to remember: Some early-stage directors may come to realize that a different skill set in their seat would be of greater value than that member can contribute. If board expansion is not feasible or practical, it may be optimal to "fire oneself" or seek a replacement representative. If investment documents require a seat for the investors, it might be time to find another partner or member of the investment group to step in with his or her unique talents.

As successful companies grow from the earlier seed-capital stage to the later venture capital stage of their growth journeys, the board must prepare for the almost inevitable expectation of larger-dollar investors to demand one or more board seats. In some cases of sizeable investments, they'll want voting control of the company.

You'll learn as you teach when on a great board.
By Gerard Miller

As the company grows, the board and its individual directors need to grow. That requires self-awareness, candid self-assessment, and ongoing board education. Some boards conduct an annual directors' self-assessment: They evaluate their own performance inside and outside the boardroom, and assess their relevant skill sets and contributions to the company's growth and productive governance processes.

A few boards engage in a 360-degree evaluation process, where members receive input and observations from others, and they rate the experience positively. However, this can be tricky. In one of my previous board experiences, the directors' unfiltered criticism of one colleague was so severe that he quit -- and we lost important industry insights over what was essentially an arrogant board member personality. Coaching and thoughtful ground rules could have reduced the friction. So proper moderation can be vital to keeping the process constructive.

One network available to companies, which is most commonly joined after they achieve profitability, is the National Association of Corporate Directors, which produces useful publications and conducts conferences and training for independent directors. NACD can provide board self-evaluation tools and CEO assessment templates, which are also available through various private firms that are readily available on-line.

Company-specific director education should also be structured into the board meeting schedule. Topics for board education can include recent technology developments, industry structure, competition, legal developments in the company's industry, and recent activity in the M & A market, to name a few. The directors themselves should identify and prioritize these topics. The reward to board members is an education that is useful within the company and in other board assignments.

These board-wide education sessions can often provide learning experiences for senior managers, board observers and advisors. But my advice is to keep the attendance limited to avoid a "theatre in the round" effect that discourages questions that could spotlight a director's ignorance of a key subject.

For individual directors, a personalized "curriculum" of learning events can be developed in conjunction with the CEO or the lead director, which may include attendance at industry conferences (where both customers and competitors are attending), and technical education programs.

Find an outside confidant, a CEO coach.

The CEO position can be a lonely place, especially when the CEO finds himself or herself in a position of not being able to bring an issue directly to the board and not wanting to explore solutions with associates within the company. This sometimes happens when a CEO is unwilling to admit a weakness in an area that is critical, such as analysis of financial statements, or when a CEO is unhappy with the actions of his board or with pay offers by the board's compensation committee that cannot be resolved amicably. Having an experienced coach, usually acting informally and not for any kind of pay, is a safety valve for a CEO that cannot be understated when in times of great stress.

Sometimes that coach is a member of the board willing to listen and make suggestions off the record. And often that is good enough. In my experience, there are times when a CEO needs a completely neutral third party or a roundtable of fellow CEOs to help guide through a difficult maze.

How would you like a great advisory board?

Have you ever thought of creating an advisory board? As you can guess, that would be an informal group with no legal responsibilities, but one able to be called upon to act as business, industry and scientific advisors to you and the company.

Usually, you would want to create an advisory board to fill in the critical areas of need not evidenced in the board of directors or within the company itself. University professors, industry gurus, lawyers familiar with patent law and former executives of competitor companies are typical recruits you might consider. Sometimes, celebrities will agree to sit on an advisory board as a gift to the CEO, providing a bit of glamour for the company at small expense.

How many advisors should you seek for a board?

There is no limit to the number of individuals for such a board, but there is a practical limit to the amount of cash and / or stock to be allocated to these outside advisors. The rule of thumb for an advisory board member is to expect a half to a full day each year on site, typically in a strategic planning meeting with numerous members of the staff, as well as some reasonable number of phone calls from senior members of management during the year. Included in the "package" is the expectation that the advisor's name will be freely used in the company's marketing, a bio listed on the website, and occasional calls will come as references to the advisor from potential investors and others looking for deeper insight into the secret sauce of the company or state of the industry than can be provided by many on the inside.

How do you pay an advisory board?

For this, an advisory board member for a small to medium sized company should expect to receive options equal to ¼% of the fully diluted stock of the company, vesting over two years, and subsequent grants if there has been additional stock issued to dilute the advisor, bringing the advisor back to this percentage if an advisor is renewed after subsequent two-year intervals. Alternatively, some companies pay an advisor a fee of $1,000 to $2500 per "on premises" meeting day and optionally much smaller stock grants, if any.

Additional commitments of time by an advisory board member should be compensated as would any consultant, at half and full day rates agreed upon in advance between the CEO and the advisor. There is no rule as to uniformity of pay, as some advisors may be willing to serve at no cost while others are industry consultants used to receiving fair payment for services rendered.

Are there any special documents needed for advisors?

Advisors fill blind spots in the corporate knowledge base and guide you in areas where you feel you have a personal weakness. There is usually a formal agreement between the company and the advisor, carefully calling out the time expectation, the forms and amounts of payment, and the indemnifications from liability granted by the company to the advisor in return for confidentiality and non-disclosure of company trade secrets by the advisor.

I sit on a board of a company with potentially valuable patents that it is exploiting aggressively. The board has hired an attorney firm to pursue protection of these patents in the courts, but the members of the board felt that it would be wise to add a member to the advisory board who is also a patent attorney to watch over the process and advise the board at its meetings of issues that may not have been covered by the paid attorney or by other member of the board itself. In this case, payment for the attorney advisory board member was agreed to in the form of common stock options more generous than the average advisory board grant, as the attorney was invited to sit in on all meetings of the corporate board and agreed to do so. There are many variants of the rule for payment, and many reasons why advisors may be willing to serve. In this instance, the attorney realizes that the potential value of the stock options in the event of major wins in patent litigation would far outweigh any fees which he might have charged.

A particularly strong advisor, especially if well known, may be named chairman of the advisory board, which is often just an honorary title, since the CEO is usually tasked with the planning of the full day meeting of advisors annually, and setting the agenda to match the needs of the corporate board and senior management.

An experienced coach has seen your movie before.

Business coaches come in all sizes and shapes. You'll have a relative willing to devote time, a school friend with business experience, professionals who charge for the service, investors with a reason to promote your success and more.

But by far the best coaches are those that have lived through the process you're going through and built successful enterprises in your same industry. Especially if they have sold their companies and live comfortably upon the proceeds, these people are often the most willing to help and are the most patient through the process.

One great source for coaches is among fellow members of a CEO roundtable organization, Young Presidents Organization, or similar association where you are comfortable with the coach candidate and know something about his or her style. Another is through industry associations or civic groups such as Rotary or Lions Club. Some larger communities have organizations of corporate directors, composed of a combination of service providers and professional corporate directors. I've personally been involved with the ABL Organization for well over thirty years and share problems and solutions with a monthly roundtable of smart CEOs from companies of all sizes.

If you take smart money from a good angel or venture organization, the lead investor usually becomes your board member and has a vested interest in your success. If you are lucky enough to create competition among investors for your company, you can select the investor or group with an individual who has experience in your niche and identifies with your vision.

How do you pay a coach? If the coach is also a significantly large investor such as a VC fund, the board member-coach will offer a limited amount of time outside of board work at no extra cost, all for the good of the investment. Professional advisors and consultants are typically paid by the half day or full day, charging anywhere from $400 per half day at the low end up to $3,000 or more at the high end for a full day of work. Some charge by the hour, making themselves available much as an attorney, keeping track of hours spent on phone calls and emails with you. And some will willingly work for stock options, an amount to be negotiated based upon time spent and stage of corporate development.

Years ago, I co-wrote my first book, profiling just such a person, trading his time and experience in exchange for equity - and managing to become wealthy in the process by picking and aiding great young companies that grew large and were ultimately sold at a tremendous profit. We had no term for such work in those days and created the phrase "resource capitalist" to describe the person and process. He brought resources to the table from personal experience to a great contact base and was able to help speed the time to market while introducing the company to great potential buyers at the right time in the process. His average percentage of a company was 5% in return for spending a day a week as I recall.

Jokingly, I used to tell people that I worked for food, with so many free lunches being offered from all sides. But alas, there is no free lunch. And over the years I have vastly curtailed the practice. However, there surely are experienced executives out there who'll work for a meal. It is worth asking.

There must be many more creative ways to pay a coach, especially for early-stage businesses. The one warning: avoid those looking to become partners, asking for larger portions of equity than, say, 5% when they contribute no cash to the enterprise. There may be times when such a person can truly be a founding partner in a young business and devote enough time and resources to warrant more, but this is taking on a partner in every sense of the word and should be done carefully and only after spending time with a number of the person's references and becoming comfortable with the person, ready for the long run.

Develop relationships with fellow CEOs in non-competing businesses for a start. Perhaps even formalize the relationship with regular lunch meetings or meetings in groups of CEOs to discuss personal issues without fear of the discussion leaking outside closed doors.

Don't forget those informal "grab a lunch" advisors.

Whether you find advisors from family, friends, faculty or fellow managers, great advisors can become an informal resource that rivals that of more formal resources, including board members. You will certainly know when you've found such a treasure, almost always through introduction by others and rarely because you have deliberately approached someone to fill a needed hole. Most of these people will provide time for you out of friendship, rather than seeking reward in the form of stock options or pay for service. Therefore, it is important that you recognize their worth and be most careful not to overuse the gift of their time. "We work for food" is a common mantra for such friends who are willing to provide such informal services.

Are there any rules for the amount of time you might expect before stepping over the line? In my experience both seeking and providing such informal services, personal visits to a company for more than a short time before or after a lunch or dinner are fine. But a scheduled visit for more than a tour and meeting management is asking too much unless offered. These people are not about the pay, and the treasure of their advice is worth the careful use of time in its seeking.

The best use of informal advisors is through phone and emailed short requests for help with a specific issue, one that can be explained easily and rather quickly, and whose resolution may be complex, but with good advice, you can find the way through the problem more quickly and even validate your intuitive answers to a problem. These informal advisors will appreciate occasional updates in the form of emails just as you would email board members with news of progress. But such contacts should never be constant or frequent.

Of course, you are free to just drift away from such resources by stopping the calls and emails, most often without being missed and therefore without a need to worry over the effect of your inaction. Such advisors, if providing concise and sage responses to questions well asked, are another valuable tool and one without a price tag.

Great relationships are among your most valuable assets.

As you follow these insights, you'll detect a continuing theme, emphasizing the need for deep and wide relationships that the CEO and senior staff can call upon for advice and guidance. This is the time to elevate those insights to the level of highest value for the corporation, one that cannot be listed on a balance sheet nor included in an appraisal of corporate worth. And yet, such relationships properly used and never overused, can quickly and precisely help a CEO cut through delays in government agencies, speed the process of product planning and ultimate release, aid in positioning in the market and help the CEO avoid a myriad of mistakes that could prove costly in time and money.

Often, I am asked by young CEOs how much time should be devoted to various types of tasks by a good CEO in a small, growing enterprise. Of course, the response depends upon lots of variables, including whether the company is in a fund-raising mode (in which case the CEO may be spending up to 80% of his or her time on this alone). I am chairman of the Technology Division of the ABL Organization, a roundtable organization with multiple CEO roundtables of about twelve members each, meeting monthly.

Each CEO is asked to make a deep presentation once a year in which he or she starts with personal and business goals for the coming year followed by concerns as to how to reach these goals. Much of the rest of the presentation is devoted to explaining to the group the causes for the concerns and offering information for the group to use in the feedback session to help the CEO seek solutions and to provide resources to the CEO for that purpose. The format also calls for the CEO to examine his calendar over a period of time and report classes of activities by percentage of total time spent, so that the group may add comments about use of CEO time to the critique. It is from over a thousand of these CEO presentations over the years that I attempt to make these generalities.

A good CEO spends at least 30% of his or her time dealing with customers, including meeting directly with customers and being involved in closing the largest deals, maintaining CEO relationships, and "sniffing" the attitudes of customers toward the company as well as exploring the needs of the customer that might be satisfied by new product development. 15% typically is spent on direct management issues such as supervision of next level subordinates. 15% might be spent networking with those in the CEO's relationship circle, including the roundtable organizations. 10% is typically spent networking with board members, usually with frequent phone calls, and preparing for board meetings. 10% is typical in exploring strategic concepts, reading about new developments in the industry and just spending quiet time contemplating opportunities.

There are many other classes a typical CEO will list for that remaining 20%, some concentrating upon time spent in meetings of all kinds, lumped together as if all meetings are of some equal value. The group often pays close attention when this happens, since it is a sign that the CEO considers meetings of all kinds a drain upon available time, and few meetings of special importance. Whatever the spread of percentages to make 100% of a CEO's time, the CEO is asked to estimate the average number of hours spent each week at or on work. Most respond with between 60 and 80 hours a week, emphasizing what you already know, that CEOs are not often 40-hour workers. But then again, in this new world of always-on communications, who is?

Boards of directors protect the corporation first.
All other board functions are secondary.

Even venture capitalists who sit on boards where they have significant investments often forget this point. They write in their investment documents that they will occupy a seat on the board for as long as they are invested in the company, thinking of this as a protection for their investment and tool for them to influence growth.

Actually, there are two legal duties of board members. They are: *the duty of care*, and the *duty of loyalty*. Everything else is a self-imposed duty or responsibility. The duty of care is to care for the corporation asset itself, not the shareholders whom they represent. Each corporation when chartered becomes a live person in the eyes of the law, independent and subject to the care of its board of directors. Shareholders such as investors are granted few rights by law. They can elect directors for their class of stock, approve mergers and acquisitions; approve increases or changes to the capital structure of the company and other more minor actions. It is the board, made up of individual members, that is responsible for the care and maintenance of the corporate person. Sometimes, there will be a conflict of interest between the people representing the various shareholder classes on a board. This happens often when one class would be quite satisfied with the outcome of a sale of the corporation because it has lower expectations of exit value and a lower cost of shares, while another later investor class would see little relative gain in a sale and veto's the proposed transaction. The duty of care is the legal responsibility of each board member and cannot be shed because the member was elected to protect a particular class of shareholder.

Second is the duty of loyalty – loyalty to the corporate person, not to the shareholders who elected the board member. Once again, there is a need to educate board members that in conflict-of-interest cases, the corporation comes first. Some investor board members are also members of boards for companies that may overlap in markets or even compete directly, although rare. Either way, I have seen many instances over the years of my board service with VCs on the board, which the VCs have had information about other firms that would be classified as confidential - that they offered at least piecemeal in a board meeting of another company where they serve. There are issues that stress the loyalty of board members such as placement of employees or recruiting of executives from firms where the VC or board member has inside knowledge. These are rare, but each stresses the duty of loyalty to the corporation on whose board they sit.

Should board members therefore withdraw and not participate in corporate planning, coaching the CEO and other issues not related to the duty of care or duty of loyalty? Of course, they should not. A board, in exercising its duty of care, must do everything it can as an entity and each member as an individual to become acquainted with the issues, problems, opportunities and threats that overhang the corporation. In fact, there is a legal concept (not a duty) of "reasonable care" that board members must meet to be protected by the insurance carried by a company for directors and officers. Reasonable care means that members deliberate issues in depth, attract expert advice when appropriate, attend meetings regularly, stay current on corporate issues and hold regular sessions of the outside directors without management present. None of these requirements are by law, but the sum of these adds to a powerful statement of commitment by board members and therefore a protection under the law when a group of shareholders sue boards or members for irresponsible actions. Most every court will side with the members of the board under the rule of reasonable care when these behaviors are in evidence.

Strategy and stewardship go hand in hand.
By Maryann Bryla

Serving on the board of a rapidly growing business is exciting, yet the position comes with responsibility and accountability. The intensity of the environment is often fueled by the reality that the company is in a race against time and its competitors. Companies have finite resources. The leadership team needs to make progress quickly to achieve profitability and warrant more funding to grow the business. This requires board members and management to simultaneously focus on both strategy and stewardship.

Many board members will find it useful to approach this situation with the following questions:

- Assuming success, what changes will we need to make to enable the business to maintain momentum, scale and adapt to the exciting challenges of growth and success?

- Assuming critical challenges or unexpected issues facing the company, what processes or structures can we put in place to help the business quickly identify, react and change to put the business back on a positive trajectory? Do we have the right people on the management team and resources to help tackle these issues?

As you work through these questions, it becomes obvious that governance and stewardship processes will support the achievement of current business goals. These processes ensure that several future scenarios are considered, and discussed, to improve the management team's ability to react and thrive.

Board-level stewardship of resources often determines the success or failure of a company. This includes oversight of C-suite leaders, challenging and shaping the strategy of the company, measuring performance, auditing results and risk management. Monitoring the company's performance metrics, cash runway and burn rate are all critical factors of success.

Not only is protecting and conserving capital an important part of good stewardship, so is managing against any wasteful erosion of capital. Good stewardship also protects intangible assets such as the company's reputation and goodwill. The board, along with senior management, must ensure that stewardship is part of the company's inner fabric and culture. When appointing and especially when reviewing performance of a CEO, a board needs to consider how much stewardship will be part of the job description and set appropriate performance metrics that can be measured.

Management teams will have their heads down, focused on the next two-week sprint on product development or landing a potential big new account that can prove their concept or cover payroll. Often, the leadership team will lose sight of some critical big picture items while lost in the urgency of day-to-day operations. The board is there to be an important sounding board for the CEO, providing strategic guidance and expertise to help maximize performance while protecting the Company from risks or reputational harm.

Start-up management teams are easily tempted to defer decisions and investments in legal, human resources, finance and other areas with an understandable but wrong assumption that "None of this will matter if the product isn't successful" - or "we can worry about that later." In those moments, it is the Board's responsibility to offer the much needed critical and strategic perspective. Don't be afraid to ask questions like, "What are we doing to protect the intellectual property we are creating?"

How bold or confrontational should a board member be?

By Maryann Bryla

To ask or not to ask, that is sometimes the question. You want to probe, reveal and learn about the business. You want to help the leadership see other options or ideas. Sometimes you just want to understand the logic or rationale behind a strategy or key decision. However, before you start interrogating an early-stage CEO like a prosecutor on Law and Order, be mindful of your role.

The board and the management team are on the same team with shared goals. A director's job is not to run the business, but rather to offer advice to the leadership team on the strategic direction of the company and day-to-day tactics of running an organization. The goal of the board's strategic advice is to coach and help the CEO to more effectively manage the business. Directors need to keep their hands out of the business and guide the leadership to achieve critical goals and milestones. Our role is to be part coach, part mentor, part friend, and always a strategic advisor while protecting our role of governance.

Second guessing a CEO, especially in front of staff, may end up undermining the CEO. Our goal is not to try to catch or challenge leadership by raising important issues or questions. Instead, we try to look around corners -while bringing our experience, expertise and perspective in a constructive manner to ensure success. Good boards want CEOs to think about multiple options and scenarios prior to making a critical business decision that may change the trajectory and even the fate of the business.

Again, with a bias toward brevity, it's wise to document the board's due diligence sessions with the CEO to demonstrate that the board fulfilled its legal obligations of *duty of care.* So, if you are going to play devil's advocate, let everybody at the meeting know why you are doing. It can be most constructive to be the one who is the "devil's advocate," asking the tough questions. Consider phrases like: "Just to play devil's advocate so we consider the alternatives, or "Just to make sure we look around the corner on this one…."

Start with trust and openness. Help the CEO know you are there to help him/her and the business be successful. How can we best do this? Think about how dolphins raise their young: They don't swim ahead, and they don't swim behind. They swim next to them. They swim with them. Yet, they protect them. They steer them with a gentle nudge. When danger appears, they take action to protect.

In most of your dealings, you can question a CEO to uncover and reveal opportunities. You can nudge, but you don't need to steer. Take a lesson from the wise dolphin!

That said, when you see danger to the company lurking around the corner, your questions need to be strong and direct. Boards need to protect business and investors' capital. There will be times when the CEO or other key leaders become the danger because the business has outpaced their abilities to manage it. We discuss that scenario in future insights.

The need for a board grows with complexity.

Start-ups with one founder rarely have or need a board of directors. In fact, such a board would seem out of place in a one-person company. As soon as any outside money is ingested into the corporation, others have a vested and legal interest in the behavior of officers entrusted with the best use of funds. Money from friends and family usually is offered in a casual manner with much less restriction than professional investors, so that a formal board is a logical step but not often created upon this event. Then along comes either money or contracts from strategic or financial investors or partners. The operations of the corporation become more complex. Ownership is spread among several classes of investors. The number of employees grows. Bank loans with restrictive covenants are taken on. These events, one or all, usually are triggers for the founders to seek to create a board for oversight and guidance.

Once created, it is logical to follow the standard practice in the creation of two standing committees composed of outside board members (not employees or executives) – the compensation committee and the audit committee. Compensation's charter is to approve stock option grants for any employee, no matter how small the grant, and all salary and benefits for at least the CEO if not the next level down, to avoid conflict of interest with the CEO. All actions of the committee are in the form of recommendations to the full board for vote and are not binding until that event.

Second, the audit committee is responsible for hiring an outside auditor as appropriate, reviewing the accounting practices of the corporation and making sure that laws are followed relating to recognition of revenues and expenses. Good audit committees also review the corporation's insurance portfolio, risk protection policies such as email and computer use, disaster response and recovery policies and any other area where the corporation's very life could be at risk from inattention.

Let me tell you the story of a company on whose board I sat for several years. The CEO insisted that between husband and wife, over half the stock always be in their hands, refusing new offerings or any other form of dilution, and controlling the majority of board seats in the process. After replacing two board members with two other friends who were a bit less independent, during that first meeting with all present including the two new board members, I suggested that the corporation then form the two committees – audit and compensation. "Never!" was the single word as I recall the CEO's immediate outburst. I made a motion to bring it to a vote. The corporate attorney was present, recommending this as a relatively safe move for the CEO. I called the question after a drifting discussion. You can guess that the three friends voted down the measure, perhaps as a sign of unison, since this was the first vote by the two new members. It was the final nail for me.

I engineered the extraction of the outside investors, even at a near total loss. At least the investors could then take the loss against ordinary income under rule 1244 of the IRS code, worth something to each, rather than being locked into what was a slowly failing lifestyle business with no effective oversight.

Did the company incorporate in the right state?
By Gerard Miller

Often, the founder's personal domicile or its original location becomes the company's legal and tax domicile, without giving much thought to whether that arrangement is optimal for the long run. The company's attorney should be able to advise a board about important litigation and tax considerations. Venture investors often find a candidate company domiciled in a state they object to considering the above and require that the company reincorporate in Delaware. But be aware, the domicile state most always requires that the company reincorporate in the home state as a "foreign corporation" which saves no state taxes, if that is the reason for such a reincorporation to Delaware. Other states such as Nevada and Wyoming have no state corporation tax, but the state in which the company does business still will want incorporation as a foreign entity.

As a newcomer to the board, you should confer with the company's legal counsel, who can provide important historical context and an honest assessment of the benefits and potential complications of the company's domicile. For example, it is often assumed that the superior domicile for national companies is Delaware: It has a long history as a corporate-friendly state in both its statutes and a long trail of litigation for which strong precedents have removed many uncertainties when litigation arises. However, a company located in the western United States, where it must also abide by state business laws where its headquarters and facilities are located, may find it less compelling to defend itself in Delaware courts. Unfortunately, this is particularly true in corporate bankruptcy cases, where Delaware is less friendly to creditors than most other states.

Other legal obligations that derive from the company's physical locations and business operations -- including the location of its customers and employees -- should be well understood by both management and the full board. These include tax considerations, state laws concerning the size and even the composition of the board, limitations on employment agreements such as non-compete clauses, labor laws, tort laws and director liability, and other important operational matters. These nuances deserve an annual agenda item to ensure that the full board is updated on important legal developments in the states where it operates, and any repositioning that should be considered. Inviting the corporate attorney to visit a board meeting for this review is just one more "best practice" in board governance.

You have some great relationships: Reach out to your networks for talent, customers and advisors
By Maryann Bryla

A director is appointed to serve on the board for many reasons, including industry and functional expertise, professional networks, investment or financial expertise and track record of success. As we've said before, the role as a board member is to be a mentor and strategic advisor, not a manager.

But there may be times when you know the best next step to help the company progress is to leverage your own diverse set of external contacts to help solve a business problem or to source critical talent. But don't be a Lone Ranger. It's prudent to first discuss your outreach ideas and options with other directors. Together you may be able to map out the known resources and an action plan that the CEO can coordinate so it doesn't' feel like a runaway board.

Clearly, discretion is required if the problems are internal or confidential. In these moments, you will define the relationship between the Board and management team for better or for worse.

New directors with investment expertise and experience in raising capital are often asked to leverage their investor network to help the company raise capital as the business grows. This is not unusual.

Many entrepreneurs may be experts in their field, but not experts in fundraising. Fundraising can sometimes look easy, yet it rarely is for most companies. Raising capital typically takes an enormous amount of the CEO's time, energy and focus. In some but not all companies, board members can thus create value by using their relationships and opening their various networks to help the company raise capital, hire top talent or bring in new customer relationships.

For board members to be willing to open their various networks, the most important currency at this time is trust. Trust among the leadership team. Trust among the members of the board. Trust with the CEO. By fostering a high trust culture between the board and management, then requests to ask your networks for help or support should not be a surprise to anyone and can build confidence as well as create significant value.

A board member who doesn't fully trust management or the company's progress toward its goals may not be willing to open their relationship doors to the CEO or management.

Fight for balance on your board.

In a recent insight, I described the CEO who stacked the board with two friends, making a majority for control purposes and relegating the investor representatives to insignificance. There were no outside board members with industry experience, no members the CEO trusted with governance backgrounds, no scientists to evaluate the technology that is the core asset of the corporation.

If the CEO does not do so, outside board members must fight for balance on the board. If for no other reason, this protects the members of the board from making decisions without rising to the standard of careful deliberation under the "reasonable care" test.

Some boards find themselves debating whether there should be an expansion from five to seven, from seven to nine or more to allow for such a mixture of protective seats created by the investment documents and balance with outside board members. Sometimes, as in one board where I sit today, there are so many classes of investors, each with one or more seats, that a seven-person board is not enough. I am not for large boards. There are social studies that reinforce the notion that a group of six or seven is far more likely to arrive at reasoned decisions effectively than larger groups. Look at the example of most non-profit boards, where the number of members often exceeds thirty, requiring the creation of an executive committee to get the work done.

Board members should be elected annually.

No board member should be grandfathered, guaranteed a board seat forever.

Practically speaking, this is an impossible goal. We have investigated the restrictions imposed by investment documents and the obvious need to keep continuity on the board with the retention of the CEO position at the very least. But it would be the best of form to require in the bylaws of a corporation that all seats are re-elected annually.

For non-profits, this allows for the creation of a board development committee to find and recruit outstanding new board members and find ways to unseat those who are no longer contributing or even attending board meetings. Such a policy further reinforces the duty of care for the corporation by its board. Unseated board members with longevity and a history of participation can be invited to become "emeriti" members of the board with observation rights but no vote.

Although not required by all corporate bylaws, all companies should hold and document an annual shareholder meeting in which the shareholders are notified at least 20 days in advance and given the right to submit a proxy vote for their choice of officers and for any other issues that will come to a vote, including expansion of the stock option plan to include more available shares.

The bottom line is that good corporate governance calls for a skill set within the board that is not often present, but for the protection of the members and the corporation itself, necessary.

Good board members are as valuable as good executives.

Perhaps this is the natural conclusion from the several insights previously explored. While the CEO and management offers the vision, strategies, and tactics as well as the proposed budget, it is the board that controls with its votes the execution of strategy, the expenditure of cash, the taking on of debt or new equity, the very direction of the company as well as its ultimate health.

The most important person in a corporation usually is and should be the CEO. This person, often the founder in early-stage companies and beyond, is the originator and keeper of the vision, leading all others below and the board above as willing believers in the vision advanced. But the board is responsible for providing resources to fulfill that vision, which may include new cash infusion or assumption of new debt.

In extreme situations, it is the board that must step up and replace the CEO, assuming the responsibility for finding and integrating a new leader quickly and efficiently. Sometimes this means having a board member step in for a short time as CEO for continuity. Recently, one of the CEOs in a roundtable who had been active and vibrant for years in both his company and the roundtable, died suddenly of a heart attack. His board met in emergency session and managed a smooth transition to a new leader within a month, during the most traumatic of times for all employees and the board itself.

For non-profit boards, the two most important duties under the duty of loyalty and care are the oversight and eventual replacement of the CEO, and maintenance of the entity over its infinitely long lifetime. I have been a member and even chair of several presidential search committees and can attest that board members (and other designated stakeholders) spend hundreds of hours in the recruiting process, all without pay.

It is because the continuity provided by the board is the one thing shareholders must count on above all else to protect investment, that the board rises in importance to at least equal stature as the executive cohort.

To you directors: Noses in, fingers out.

I first heard this years ago in a governance seminar for a non-profit higher educational board upon which I sit. It made an impact and stuck with me through the years. I have repeated it often to boards deliberating action and to individual board members seeking to get their hands dirty inside the corporation by giving advice and helping at levels beneath the CEO.

The problem cannot be overstated. Once a board member reaches beyond the CEO into the corporation, especially without the approval of the CEO, Incurable damage has been done to the CEO's ability to govern. Even if not the intent, there is an instant change in dynamic once this line has been crossed.

There is even a gray area that illustrates this effectively. As chairman of a company in an industry where I have extensive experience, I elected to attend a regular meeting of the management team with its middle managers on a Monday morning, a practice I had not done in the past. The meeting was tame to say the least. The CEO spoke, shared metrics, spoke of issues to be addressed during the coming week, and did a fine job of pointing the assembled troops in the right direction. I could not have been more pleased.

After returning to my office, I received a call from the CEO. 'Would I please (oh, don't take this wrong, Dave) not attend these meetings anymore?' What I took for unusual silence was a complete disruption of the normal give and take of the management group because of my presence. The chairmanship carries unstated power even if not overtly demonstrated, since the CEO reports to and is accountable to the board, and of course its chair. I learned from this that there are times when members of the board are appropriately brought into an operating group, and certainly times when the board should hear from vice presidents presenting their issues in a board meeting. But the position of CEO is absolutely to be reinforced at all costs, never to be undermined by any member or by the board as an entity.

Therefore, it is appropriate to ask tough questions, request help in understanding issues, seek permission from the CEO to interview others. But a board member should never react to statements heard by issuing directions or hints of board action in return. It is appropriate to state that the board member understands much more after the briefing and will be able to address the problem with the board and CEO. It is not appropriate for a board member to promise any action to anyone beneath the level of CEO. Noses in; fingers OUT.

How about your board meetings? Schedules and attendance matter.
By Marryann Bryla

Most boards meet on a quarterly basis while some early-stage companies may operate on a monthly or bi-monthly schedule. One of the best things a board can do to ensure success is to establish basic operating principles.

The board exercises the powers and duties provided in the company's certificate of incorporation or bylaws. The first step in getting organized is for the board to meet on a regular basis. These meetings should follow a consistent agenda that includes a forum for discussion of long-term objectives, business strategies, acquisitions, fundraising activities and any legal matters.

Attendance matters. When you accept an invitation to serve as a new director on a board, your top obligation is to attend meetings. A company's bylaws will typically include provisions to reach quorum-- the minimum number of board members necessary to vote at a meeting before any business can be transacted legally. Many decisions made by the board and leadership are time sensitive such as approving budgets, fundraising activities and acquisitions. If there is an attendance issue with the board, it must be taken seriously so the company can progress. It's rare, but sometimes directors need to ask a chronic absentee to step down. Attendance should be a basic item in the board's annual self-evaluation.

A regular meeting calendar, with a consistent yet adaptable agenda, helps to focus new leadership teams. The meetings then become a forcing function to measure progress and accountability. This is just one way that good boards refine and focus the work of a leadership team on the things that matter most.

Regular meeting schedules benefit the company in two other ways: they help the board ensure proper governance is in place and enable the CEO to perform at a higher strategic level through effective decision making required to achieve important milestones.

Agendas frame the key discussions. Minutes foster accountability.

By MaryAnn Bryla

Agendas and meeting minutes are much more than administrative recordkeeping. An agenda sets the tone and outlines the purpose for the meeting, along with what tasks the board must accomplish. Board agendas should be circulated prior to each meeting to set clear expectations. This allows members time to prepare. Preparation helps increase member engagement and fosters a more strategic, proactive board when addressing emerging business problems. Being proactive most often yields better results than being reactive. Board members are often highly skilled, busy, organized professionals with limited time. A thoughtful agenda will value and help optimize time and increase the efficiency of decision making.

Board agendas frame the board meeting timetable and topics to be discussed. The topics on the agenda will include performance of the business, including Key Performance Indicators (KPIs), budget review, and performance vs. budget. Agendas often include executive sessions, to signal expectations for observers and staff to plan to exit the meeting, as well as to allow for discussion of confidential matters that will be off record from board minutes.

Agendas and meeting minutes assure accountability. For a leadership team in an early-stage environment, it is easy and often well intentioned to be enthusiastic about what goals the team will achieve. The meeting conversation can be exciting and dynamic, and everyone involved leaves feeling good and optimistic about the meetings. However, without practical and high-quality challenging discussions, these exciting board conversations evaporate as soon as the participants leave the room. The leadership team goes back to the routine of running the business operations and the board goes back to their many other responsibilities.

The real danger here is that months and quarters can slip by without discussion and refinement of action plans, results, measurements and, ultimately, accountability. Keeping a written record of every board meeting and performance against goals is important to hold management accountable for commitments and board members accountable for their discussions and oversight. Some boards keep a separate "action item" document to remind members of tasks promised but not yet complete.

The board must select a qualified person to fill the role of board secretary, whose responsibility is to take the minutes of each board meeting. The board secretary will draft the minutes to document the most important discussions, board votes, follow-up action items, as well as recording attendance and attainment of a quorum. The Board minutes are not meant to record all the details of the meeting, rather only the most important topics, decisions and votes which then become part of the official corporate record. Board minutes can provide protection to the board for carrying out their fiduciary duties.

Once the minutes are completed, they are circulated to each board member for review and approval. After the board approves the final board minutes, they formally become part of the corporate record and can be used for historical reference and accountability.

A final thought: board minutes are discoverable in a lawsuit. So, it is important to document only the subjects discussed, not the details. You will find that non-profit board minutes almost always go the opposite direction, with a detailed account of each discussion, sometimes naming members contributing and even those who made and seconded motions. Do not confuse this with company or corporate board minutes.

Feed your board with constant care and attention.
Plan 10% of your time for board relations.

Most all leaders new to the CEO position underestimate this time requirement. It is good for the company when the CEO shares concerns, threats and opportunities with the board. The rule of "no surprises" works well for the longevity of a CEO. But there are always surprises. CEOs should communicate with members of the board if not a committee of the whole as soon as possible when threats to the corporation arise.

Sometimes the CEO wants to obtain concurrence from his board for issues of particular importance to him. It is not bad form to lobby individual board members in the form of a briefing of the issue as the CEO sees it, if the board is allowed the time to debate the issue, sometimes requesting an "executive session" of just the outside directors.

All this board management is time-consuming. The CEO is also responsible for preparing the board briefing package before regular board meetings, a time-consuming task if done correctly. The package should contain the issues to be discussed with backup materials for the board to understand the issues. Operating statistics in detail and individual departmental issues that do not rise to the level of board discussion should be included only in an appendix for deeper reading, but not discussion. The CEO should discuss the agenda and board package contents with the chairman (if the chair is a different person), since the chair is tasked with setting the agenda and controlling the meeting.

Does this not appear to add to at least 10% of a CEO's time now that you've seen some of the elements of the task?

How about communication and obligations to Investors?

By Maryann Bryla

People do not like uncertainty. Financial markets do not like uncertainty. Investors do not like uncertainty.

see this play out through the eyes of investors, imagine the following: As an angel investor, you invest $1 million dollars of your hard-earned money into a company. You are excited about the Company's leadership team and the investment. However, many months pass by without an update. When you finally get an update, the report lacks critical performance numbers (KPIs) and other financial information. This is a bad scenario for all. To avoid this, the board should set the tone with the CEO for developing a proactive *best-in-class* investor reporting process.

Early on, especially with early-stage companies, the CEO will have exciting things to communicate to investors, and it will be easy. In challenging times, the temptation will come to change, filter, or omit things when the numbers aren't what the leadership wants to share.

Regular and timely reports to investors should acknowledge shortfalls to avoid surprises. If a Company fails to report surprises, there could be significant consequences including the erosion of trust and confidence in the leadership of the company. Once trust is broken with investors, the Company's ability to raise additional funding could be negatively affected in the investment community, even if the overall business is going well.

A Company's leadership team must communicate realistic expectations to investors. For example, "You will get a quarterly letter from our CEO with updates about the people, products and performance in our company, along with a quarterly financial update. A CEO who does this will build trust and confidence with the investor base by communicating on a regular basis. By doing so, the CEO increases the chances that investors will choose to fund the Company again in the future.

Those investors will also be far more understanding and supportive if the business has an issue or is forced to pivot. On the other hand, if existing investors are left in the dark by a CEO, management and the board should not expect a bailout or rescue capital. So, the board clearly has a role to play here: it's not just the CEO's prerogative. Experienced investors are warried and tired of hearing from a CEO or company only when in need of additional cash.

One more caveat here: CEOs should preview investor communications with the Board of Directors to ensure they are effectively and clearly communicating accurate company performance indicators without inadvertently releasing confidential company data. Getting extra eyeballs on these messages is worth the extra day it may require to vet proprietary information. A CEO cannot assume investors will keep company information confidential despite non-disclosure agreements (NDAs) and investor pledges to do so.

D&O insurance is a "cost of respect" for board members.

Whenever there are outside shareholders, and when there is a product in release, there is a chance, no matter how slight, of a lawsuit against members of the board as well as against the corporation itself. Even if such a suit is completely without merit, the cost of defense and the risk of a negative outcome both hang over the company and the director. Directors and Officers insurance is meant to reduce that risk and provide for the legal defense of any such suit at the expense of the insurance company. In that regard, even the lowest amount of D&O insurance available, $1 million, provides for legal defense costs to be covered. The usual cost for such insurance is $4 to $6 thousand a year, with an extra $2 thousand for an additional million of coverage.

More important than the cost is the provision of investment documents from sophisticated investors requiring D&O insurance for the company at the time of funding.

Over the many years of board service, I have been sued as a director several times, in no case covered under the umbrella of a D&O policy. Although I won each of these rather spurious suits, the cost of defense in some of the cases was not reimbursed, and the time spent helping the attorney prepare for the defense and in one case through to a several day adjudication event, was not small. As a result, I now insist upon D&O insurance for every board upon which I sit. The backgrounds of these suits make for good stories but are not appropriate for this telling.

Here's a rule that can "save" a board!
By Gerard Miller

It's called the "business judgment rule. " It's a principle in corporate law that generally protects directors and officers of a corporation from legal liability if they act with "due care." Historically the rule arose through the courts and not the legislatures, going back conceptually to an English court decision in 1742, and then cited in 1829 in Louisiana in *Percy v Millaudon*, where a bank's shareholders unsuccessfully sued the directors for misconduct. There have been numerous US court cases where a board was saved from a shareholder suit because it proved that it followed the business judgment rule.

Now, do we have your attention?

The idea is that even though directors may be held guilty of acts of commission or omission, malfeasance or non-feasance, their decisions and the board members themselves should *not* be legally exposed to breaches of trust or misconduct -- if their acts are executed legally, within their authority, and with reasonable care. The *Percy* court specifically held that directors should not be liable for mistakes in judgment "if the error was one into which a prudent man might have fallen." That court went on to admonish that to avoid liability, directors must act with "fidelity and reasonable diligence." These rulings gave birth to the key concepts of the "duty of loyalty" and the "duty of care" which we'll cover later in this book.

Thus, it is important that the board minutes discussing such important issues, including whether to accept an acquisition or make one, should reflect the fact that the board spent considerable time discussing the issue before coming to a conclusion. And of course, there must have been such a discussion in depth as protection under the rule.

Where the board instructs management to take certain actions in conditions of considerable uncertainty or risk, it's a good idea to have corporate counsel review the minutes to assure that the way such actions are documented will be helpful and not hurtful if things go sour. On one of my previous company boards, a wealthy director was adamant that his dazzlingly insightful and luminous comments should be preserved for all posterity, until a year later a friend in his elite circle shared with him the disaster story of how her company's board minutes were subpoenaed and used against her in a lawsuit. He quickly reversed himself, insisting that corporate counsel pre-scrub the minutes thereafter, advocating then that they contain only a level of documentation thus deemed "necessary and sufficient" for legal defense. This story is a great lesson for all boards.

Be sure the Board and CEO are in alignment.
By William De Temple

Boards of directors have the power to hire and fire the CEO, even if the CEO is the founder of the company. That's not only a daunting prospect, but it is one that can result in more than just misunderstandings between board members and the founder of a company.

Sometimes, because this very issue could destroy or damage an enterprise, it is most important to understand and prevent. Here's a true story that will scare any founder taking money from third parties. But don't be too afraid to read this. We'll have some insights into prevention in just a bit.

The company CEO worked hard for three years and developed strong relationships with nine major retailers nationwide for a series of new products which had a quick return on investment of between nine and twelve months. There was over $2 million of angel capital invested in the company, with the entrepreneur-CEO initially investing several hundred thousand of his own money.

The company's new products were patented, and they were completing beta tests at user sites from which the company had received its first order for just over $65 million, based on an expected three-year roll out.

An angel investor who had a seat on the board concluded that the entrepreneur-CEO didn't have the experience necessary to take the company through what appeared would be the rapid growth curve about to come. At the next board meeting, without any prior notice or discussion, he proposed replacing the entrepreneur with a mature, seasoned CEO - completely blindsiding the entrepreneur and the rest of the board. After hearing the board member make his case, the board agreed with him that the entrepreneur-CEO did not appear to have the experience necessary - and voted to replace him.

Removed and shaken, the founder-CEO initiated suit, and both parties ultimately agreed to binding arbitration. The advocate board member even argued during arbitration that the entrepreneur's share of the company was unreasonably high and requested a redistribution of ownership of the company.

Somehow ignoring terms of the investment agreements, the arbitrator ruled in favor of the investors, and affirmed the board's decision. The entrepreneur lost control of the company and his job in the company he founded. A new mature, seasoned president was brought in to manage the company as planned by the board. That would be the end of the story if not for a subsequent event.

The board failed to consider the strength of the relationships built over the years between the entrepreneur and the company's major customers. The advocate board member was elected chairman of the board and took on the responsibility of negotiating the terms of an employment agreement with the new president. However, the two were never able to agree on the final terms of that employment agreement, in spite of the new CEO already starting work.

At the local airport, on their way to a major meeting with a customer preparing to enter into a significant contract, the new CEO demanded that the chairman sign the employment agreement he thought he had negotiated, or he was not getting on the flight. The chairman refused to sign "with a gun to his head," and the CEO never got on that flight. The contract with the major new customer was never executed. Word spread through the retail community. The original retailer cancelled its $65 million order. The company soon closed its doors.

What went wrong here? First, there was no orderly discussion of the issues between the advocate board member, the full board, and the entrepreneur. Properly presented, the entrepreneur might have concurred with the position for the sake of increasing value of his own founder stock. Properly handled, the board might have granted the entrepreneur the continued position of chief visionary, head of business development, or any title and responsibility that would have best served the company and its needs. With that, he might have been happy to step aside and add a seasoned CEO to the company, for the benefit of his equity value and that of all others. Instead, the confrontation destroyed all good will between the founder and the board, making a sharing of knowledge and transfer of customer relationships impossible.

Second, no one on the board role-played the effect of the decision upon the customer community or planned how to handle the transition in its many forms, including ongoing contract negotiations.

There are times when a transfer of power is an emergency or is strategically vital to complete with a precise and very sharp knife. This was not one of those, and the company suffered the ultimate loss of value as a result of that decision not to seek an orderly transition.

There is a message here for boards of directors and entrepreneur-founders. It is always best to communicate early when there are concerns and find a way to achieve mutual goals in the best way possible, even at the expense of some duplication of effort and payment of additional cash during a transition. There are almost always ways to reduce the emotional impact upon the one most affected by such an action. And it is always best for all to avoid the costs and stress of litigation.

Product-market fit: An important board subject for growth or survival
By Gerard Miller

One of the frequent reasons for failures by startups is product-market fit. Board members cannot insert themselves into marketing operations, but they can help the CEO and the management team point themselves in the right direction. Importantly, boards can help make sure that scarce, limited resources are deployed where they can maximize sales, revenues and profitability.

Most early-stage companies' board meetings should include a marketing update that includes product-market fit, product revisions, an update on beachhead markets, what's been learned from the field sales efforts. Reports to the board should include sales metrics including the pipeline and funnel, cycle times, hit ratios, and expected closings in coming months. The all-important cash runway will be critically affected by these factors. However, it is very easy to overdo this with detailed discussions prospect-by-prospect, which is not appropriate for a board's use of time.

CEO or senior executive reports about the competition should be concise and not devolve into the details of each, unless the company is under attack and the threat to the corporation is real.

From time to time, the board should hear directly from the chief marketing or sales executive invited into the meeting for this purpose. Management should include key performance indicators in the advance reading materials and excursions from the norm should be discussed by the board.

If a company adviser has expertise in this dimension of the company's operations and its marketplace, that advisor should be included in some of the review sessions. Where appropriate, the board members can identify one specific dimension of the marketing and sales effort on which they would appreciate a "board education and drill-down" session. Several of my previous board chairs have invited independent industry analysts and even a consultant from the buy-side to help them (and in one case, the management team) better understand the competitive landscape. Some board chairs even invite a sales rep to explain to them the lay of the land at ground zero, so that directors better understand the challenges in the field. Again, too much detail detracts from the time, spirit and effectiveness of a board.

Experienced marketing and sales managers already know that their board directors and their advisors can be valuable sounding boards. Very few products and services are so good that they sell themselves, and competition is almost always inevitable, so the board's best use is to help management through board member expertise or guidance.

Be a detective: Watch for early warning signs and signals.

By Maryann Bryla

Board members of an early-stage company don't have the same volume and history of financial performance information and metrics that prevail in more established companies. Leaders of early-stage companies in particular must measure execution on a month over month basis as the company operates. So, the few financial numbers and key performance data points you do have will each carry a great deal of value.

Since capital is limited, you won't have the luxury to wait over a year to analyze the company's performance versus plan. Although success and progress aren't perfectly linear, early misses on sales shortfalls and other key performance metrics must be taken very seriously. Entrepreneurs will often find their biggest competition is time because a company is usually burning through investment capital every day.

Here are some questions to ask about early misses:

- Do we have a forecasting and expectations problem, or a more serious business problem?
- Did we have a realistic forecast or plan to start with?
- Do we have an accurate understanding of the operating environment?
- Do we have the right strategy?
- Are we effectively executing our strategy?
- Are we providing the right resources to achieve our plan?
- Is there an issue with the performance of the product or software?

It's important to consistently measure performance results versus plan.

After measuring our results, if you realize that the corporate strategy is not fully working, a good board would provide feedback and take corrective action. The board needs to communicate clear corrective measures and ensure that leadership has committed to immediately take appropriate and effective action.

The leadership team may need a push to change what is not working and pivot if necessary. We all know that mistakes and misses will happen. As a famous investor once said, "We try to avoid making the same mistake, but the mistake family has many cousins." So, if they aren't addressed with thoughtfulness and urgency, the issue will likely repeat itself, resulting in wasted capital and corporate resources.

When a management team begins a streak of missed financial and sales goals, don't just be passive and hope for the best. Hope is not a strategy.

It is uncommon for fence-sitting or passive boards to see the business turnaround without a great deal of pain. Additionally, if a CEO continues to miss realistic goals, the board and the rest of the leadership team may begin to lose confidence. This situation underscores the need for a board to have a CEO performance plan in place first and a succession plan in place second, to effectuate a leadership transition if it's needed.

Any advice can be worthless, or worse.

Let me tell you the story of the first investment made by a newly organized formal group of angel investors. It was thrilling for these angels to find a young entrepreneur with an idea for a business that seemed so destined for greatness that the angels invested over $1 million on the condition that the group receive two board seats and one observer seat on the start-up's board. The young, eager entrepreneur agreed immediately, and the business was launched, well-funded and anticipating great profits.

As the business expanded into a second city and then planned expansion into a third, there was a rift that became evident between these angel board members, played out in front of the CEO. The angels argued about whether the expansion was too quick, requiring additional money, or should be slower and bootstrapped with profits from the first city's success. Finally agreeing upon expansion at speed, the angels raised more money and encouraged the CEO to accelerate the expansion, which the CEO did with enthusiasm. It did not take long for the company to again run out of money, and for the board to split over the next moves (since the first city continued to be profitable).

The angel investors could not raise the next, larger round to finance the shortfall and further expansion, putting the fragile young company at risk for following the advice of its board. In the end, the company had to turn to a wealthy individual investor who took control of the corporation as his price for saving the company. Had the angel board members been able to agree upon a financeable strategy for growth, the company might have been immensely successful. To put an ending to this story, the entrepreneur followed the suggestions of the new investor just as he had the angels, and accelerated quickly into more cities, again running out of cash. The wealthy investor in the meantime, unknown to the CEO or the board, ran into personal trouble with real estate investments, and could not make good on his promise to further fund the company, which found itself unable to meet its obligations and ultimately was shut down, causing a complete loss for all. Bad advice taken by an enthusiastic and compliant young CEO was the root of the cause, compounded by circumstance.

The lesson is for any CEO to filter all advice through the strainer of good reason, taking that which seems reasonable and rejecting that which is wrong for the company or the times. By not putting up any argument and being completely compliant, the CEO ceded control of the company to outsiders who gave bad advice.

Guard the Gold.

Use stock options and warrants to pay for service only rarely.

Earlier, I stated that stock options are the currency of early-stage business. This truth is obvious when a start-up has no cash. For this insight, we will assume a business is perhaps well beyond start-up and growing, but that cash is tight, used for growth and for working capital as earned. There are times when the services of others are available for stock instead of - or in addition to cash. Such service providers as web designers, public relations firms, even venture banks granting loans, often offer higher value services for a lesser amount of cash and some amount of stock options or warrants (written promises to sell stock at a set price for a future period in time).

When assessing the relative merit of using attractive non-cash forms of compensation for outside services, first be aware of the true value of your stock. Because the valuation is now a requirement under Rule 409a of the Internal Revenue Code, most companies with stock option plans today have fairly valued common stock with known prices per share. Second, when making such a decision, assess the speed of growth and risks associated with that growth, as both would affect the value of the common stock. If an imminent fund-raising effort will be undertaken and the corporate growth is slow, it is logical to fear that the next round will be dilutive and perhaps at a lower valuation than the current value per share. But if the growth is strong enough to anticipate increasing stock valuation over time, then the grants of stock instead of cash for services may in the end prove to be quite expensive to the existing shareholders by involuntarily diluting their holdings. It is the same logic larger corporations use when deciding whether to use cash or stock to make an acquisition. If the stock is highly priced, corporations may be quite willing to use their shares as currency for acquisitions. Such an analysis is in the service of all shareholders.

And remember, any grant of shares or options must be approved by the corporate board before issuance, since it changes the capital structure of the corporation, even if the option pool has been previously approved by the shareholders and board.

Do you always follow the advice of your board?

This may be news, but boards of directors can offer bad advice. A typical board is composed of five people in a company that has received outside funds from professional investors. Two members usually represent the founders or management, two are from the investors, and one is often elected by the four to represent the industry in which the company works.

Financial investors typically have deep experience running companies, often in other industries. The fifth board member often is an expert, but not an executive with operational experience. Realizing that this description is a generalization that fits some, but not all, growing firms, the dynamics of the board are a key component in the effectiveness of advice and leadership given by the board.

It is not uncommon for the founders or executives on a board to defer to the three outside board members, responding to questions and defending previous actions. All this is proper to the extent that the two founders or executives do not leave their brains at the door when attending a board meeting, acceding to the suggestions of board members as if each were a direction or order.

I still recall vividly the board of a young company that was composed of the entrepreneur and four investors, each of whom had differing thoughts on how to use resources to grow the company, giving mixed signals to the entrepreneur who wanted greatly to please each and all. That company embarked upon an expansion drive before perfecting the operation in its first city, as a result of the board's direction to the entrepreneur, which was against his better judgment although he remained relatively quiet and certainly compliant. "The board knows best" is not always true. And in this case, the company over-expanded, did not have the resources to fix problems at its new remote offices, and died a slow death from issues of control and quality, all of which might have been mitigated had the company spent more time debugging the first-city operation.

A good board deals with what and why, not how.

Who is responsible for the vision that drives the company? This is arguably the primary job of the CEO, with agreement from the board. Many entrepreneurs after taking outside investment defer to their board for matters of direction that include setting the vision, as well as executing the plan.

Here is a general rule: The CEO sets sails and points the ship, creating the vision for the company. The board provides input into that vision, testing it against their experience and reason, and challenges it as a part of its duty to protect the shareholders and care for the corporate asset. The board then assures that management receives or has resources to affect the vision, monitoring progress at each step.

The board does not get involved in *how* the job is done, but rather *why* it should be done and perhaps *when* it should be completed. Once the members, unless invited in a consulting role, involve themselves in the execution of the plan, management is robbed of its principle responsibility – execution of the plan approved by the board. When that happens, even a good CEO will pause and defer to the board before making strategic operational decisions, slowing the progress, perhaps endangering the company, by allowing competition to gain ground, and sometimes ceding some control to board members who are remote from the operation and may not be the wisest of advisors in each situation.

What if the CEO is the problem?
By Gerard Miller

When agreeing to serve on a board, most directors place their confidence in the CEO, because nobody in their right mind wants to spend months on end trying to paint stripes on a leopard or changing horses midstream. Life is too short.

But a substantial number of early-stage companies eventually evolve to a place where one or more members of the board come to suspect, and eventually become convinced, that the CEO is not best suited to provide the leadership and ongoing management of the company.

In your first year of service, you, as a new director, should verify whether the CEO has already established a formal performance evaluation process with the board, to provide opportunities for candid self-assessment, objective performance metrics assessments, and formal feedback from the independent directors. There is no excuse for not doing this.

In some cases, these discussions may reveal a blind spot in the CEO's oversight of key personnel, which requires a board level discussion of how best to coach the CEO for that deficiency. This calls for candid discussions about a remedial performance improvement plan that is expected to put the team back on track. Usually, the independent chair or a lead director is assigned follow-up responsibilities, to report back to the full board.

Where a board consensus develops that the CEO is irreconcilably the problem, and a replacement will be necessary, the directors need to confer privately about their next steps. Do they have a logical successor in mind? Will one of them step into an interim CEO role? Have they reviewed employment agreements and corporate bylaws that may govern how they must proceed? How will they best communicate with the CEO? If the company itself is now at risk, is sale to an acquirer an option, with only a placeholder at the helm? When should corporate or independent counsel become involved?

Most investor directors have seen a movie like this before in their prior professional lives, so the important task at hand at this point is to make sure that all the most important questions and issues are addressed and not overlooked. Legal protections are often to be considered, since angry former CEOs sometimes sue the board for any of several reasons -- usually emotional ones as opposed to legal issues.

In some cases, the CEO engages in a helpful dialogue about the next steps. Where the executive has honest self-awareness and a cooperative attitude as a major company investor, it may be possible to arrange for a highly professional transition with full cooperation of the displaced executive. Conversely, where it has already become obvious that such a scenario is impossible, the board must be prepared for both unpleasantries and possibly litigation. Then it is vital that the directors have developed a clear plan of action and lined up the necessary resources to protect both the company and them.

One board function: Assessing, shaping, and coaching the management team
By Maryann Bryla

Assessing, guiding and coaching the CEO are a critical part of the board's primary governance responsibilities. This assessment process gives the board members the opportunity to evaluate the CEO's performance and provide constructive feedback in key areas including annual performance goals, leadership qualities and accomplishments and challenges.

Effective boards evaluate the CEO annually focused upon the management of the team and the achievement of clearly defined strategic goals. The evaluation process ensures that the strategic direction set by the board is aligned with the CEO's capabilities. This assessment is based heavily upon the responsibilities in the CEO's job description and agreed upon goals frequently tied to the CEO's compensation. Establishing and communicating clear expectations are foundational to a good working relationship between the CEO and the board.

A holistic evaluation of the CEO's effective performance will typically include performance targets related to strategy, financial performance, working with the board, leadership/management of the team and various personal qualities such as communication skills. These performance evaluations should be held in executive session, where the board can be candid with the CEO, addressing a holistic 360 performance review, candid feedback and coaching the CEO.

Ideally, the board will facilitate a continuous improvement process. Ongoing advice and constructive commentary from the board is critical for a CEO's success. Smart CEOs often ask for occasional informal board input on "How am I doing, and what can I do better?" during executive sessions. The smarter ones are self-aware enough to be specific on areas where they need and value your insights.

Various inputs and data should be collected at regular periods of time to inform the board on the CEO's performance vs. targets. Staff presentations at board meetings should be encouraged for observing the CEO on the job and their leadership style. Ask probing questions during those meetings or executive sessions to follow. Are the employees getting the support and resources they need to achieve their growth objectives?

If the board sees red flags, they can provide constructive feedback to the CEO to shortstop any performance issues as they arise. Early Intervention is key. It is always best to communicate early when there are issues or concerns.

The Board sets a tone of trust and openness, to ensure when any problems or performance issues arise, they are dealt with quickly and effectively. The common ingredient in all these interactions is trust. The most effectively run boards are characterized by openness, trust, and collaboration.

The Board must create the best environment possible for the business to succeed. While the Board's role is to ask insightful, strategic and tough questions, the leadership must believe that the Board will not meddle in the business, or they may begin to filter key information from the Board.

What to do with a dysfunctional board.

It happens. Boards are elected by the shareholders, sometimes with preferred shareholders holding seats by right of their investment. In that instance, often the investor selects the board member and the CEO goes along with the choice, mostly out of having no alternative at the time.

Then there comes the first - or better yet the fourth - meeting of the board following the appointment of a new member. Remember that the board must by law be acting completely on behalf of the best interests of the company, not the investors, in all deliberations of the board. For the first several meetings, all parties usually play nice as they get to know the company and each other.

Some board members come to the table with preconceived notions about the capabilities of current management. We have explored this in previous insights. With this insight, we are dealing with board members who are dominant, obviously hushing their peers and often interrupting, or those always anxious to change the subject to their own agenda during meetings, including challenging management by attacking individuals (called *argumentum ad hominem*), rather than their ideas and statements. And some board members are just bullies, alienating the rest in a single sentence or meeting.

If you have never experienced such a board with members out of sync and out of sorts with each other or the rest, you have been lucky. But you have missed one of the great challenges of your business career, depending upon the importance of the board, the size of the company, and the immediacy of decisions resulting from these events.

If you are the chairman, the CEO or lead director, it is your responsibility to return the group to the core issue and even move to another agenda item if running the meeting. And if that does not work, temporarily adjourn the meeting to speak individually (and alone) with the offending board member out of earshot of the others. Describe how the actions of that person affect you and how you see them harming the board itself. If you get nowhere and you believe your cause to be just and perhaps representative of the group, return to the meeting and air the problem out with the entire board.

What if the person continues with his or her personal agenda or continues to disrupt? I have had this experience more than once. The solution I chose was to approach the VC, or another partner of the angel group, and explain the problem. I would do this only if the problem was seen in consensus by the rest of the board. In one instance, this brought about a replacement board member much more attuned to the duties and culture of the corporation. In the other, the offending board member did back off in subsequent board meetings.

Designated board seats cannot be changed because of investment documents. In the worst of situations, you might ask another partner of the investment firm for an alternate board member. For non-designated board seats the solution may be to propose a slate of board candidates without the offending person to present to shareholders for a vote at the next annual meeting, if board members are elected annually. Alternatively, it is effective - even if confrontational and emotional - to just ask the board member to step down and allow for another to be elected. And if that person is the CEO, the board will find a more effective solution not at all to the liking of the CEO. That too has happened in my board career.

In one extreme case, I was a member of a public board whose members could not agree on anything substantial, each claiming that the value of the company would be damaged in the market by proposed actions. In this case, the board was not held together by a strong chairman or CEO. I felt it my duty to suggest, then strongly support, discussions about merging with another company, which the board ultimately did. In a merger, egos sometimes dictate who survives at the board level (and at the CEO level), and offending board members from one company are rarely retained.

Board members can be very professional in comportment and in their exercise of their duties. Or not. Putting up with bullies, or those with obvious conflicting agendas not in the best interest of the company, is a step toward mediocrity.

Use your board's "golden contacts."

Boards of directors have several important functions, both legal and structural. Boards provide or see to it that there are resources for the company (especially money) to operate. The board selects, monitors, helps, and oversees compensation for the CEO. The board can replace an underperforming CEO. The board is responsible for approval of all deferred compensation for all employees at all levels, such as stock option grants, and is responsible for the vision and strategies for growth and protection of the corporate asset.

The CEO has every right to expect his or her board to help with issues when asked, particularly when board members have associates, friends, or contacts that they believe would be able to help solve a problem or provide a service requested or needed by the CEO.

We used to call these contacts collectively the "golden Rolodex," but long since have had to replace the name since there is an entire generation of management unfamiliar with the circular Rolodex. (No, that is not the watch company, if you are one of those.) Board members each have a collection of associates who, because of their relationship to the board member, usually would be willing to help provide a solution to a problem when called upon.

It is one of the most useful services some board members perform in any organization. Because of the value of these contacts to the board member, it is important that these contacts not be misused by the CEO, and that each offer is followed up with at least a first contact when a name is offered.

Some of your board members will have and offer more relevant contacts than others, and you will soon learn the importance of keeping those board members in closer contact and better informed between meetings. The intangible resources they provide can easily lead to finding ways to reduce time and cost to market, to find valuable new employees, and to find new customers who will listen to your pitch because of their relationship with the board member. People you could not reach yourself are sometimes quite willing to listen and help because of those relationships. So use the board for outreach. As long as not overused, your board members expect to be asked to offer and to encourage use of their valuable contacts.

Separate the chairmanship from the CEO position.

More and more today, shareholder organizations recommend that the positions of chairman and president (or CEO) be split, so there are checks and balances at the board level in the leadership. This recommendation is true for all companies with outside investors who are active and have or seek board representation.

If we examine the blowups that have been so public these past years in public company leaders exceeding their reasonable authority or exercising dictatorial authority to the ultimate detriment of the shareholders, in most cases the CEO and chairman was the same person. When you combine that fact with the relative inaction by the board, it becomes clear that some boards are hand-picked by the CEO who is also the chairman, and those boards are the ones most likely not to challenge marginal or bad decisions.

With a balanced chairmanship and CEO separation, the chairman sets the meeting agenda, manages the meeting, allows for asking the tough questions by board members, encourages all to speak and hopefully gain consensus, and moves the meeting along to cover critical issues. The CEO is given much of the meeting by the chairman, but it should be clear who is in charge of board meetings.

There are two types of chairmanships: executive (paid and full time) and non-executive, the latter typical of most corporations whether private or public. Non-executive chairmen (chairwomen) should actively dialog with the CEO before the meeting to discuss the agenda and expand time for discussion of critical issues. Without this, it is typical that board meetings seem to follow an agenda that does not change much from meeting to meeting, and strategic issues are often ignored at the board level when a high profile, large ego combined chair-CEO is in charge.

There is no shareholder vote required to split the positions. Officers are elected by the board, not the shareholders. So it is the responsibility of a great board to explore then act upon this recommendation from the various shareholder advocacy groups, and split the positions.

Can you just tell little business lies?

"He's not in right now." "I am going to the doctor at that time." "I paid only two dollars a unit to your competitor." Whether not true and used to avoid hurting someone's feelings, or whether used to gain an advantage in a negotiation, these little business lies are acceptable because they achieve their intended result without actually hurting the other party. Right?

Wrong - in the long run, even if apparently harmless at the moment. One problem, as demonstrated in so many movie scripts, is that you sometimes need to tell another lie to cover the first, and then another. And small lies turn into habits. And habits define the individual and often the culture of the individual's direct world of influence.

What if you are never caught telling these little business lies? Is there any harm? Sometimes you will never know that you were caught. Someone sees you at another event when you told them you were out of town. Another asks his competitor if they really did sell to the company at such a low price. Someone you told was doing a superb job and was soon fired mentions the comment to his attorney or perhaps just as damning – to former peers still in the company.

It takes only one instance of being caught to cause an entire group of people to question the truthfulness of all your statements. And that is a large consequence to come from a small business lie.

So, would you tell such white lies if you knew you'd never be caught? Never? That depends upon how you choose to live with yourself. It certainly is difficult to be truthful or silent but never slip into little lies.

For much of my adult life, I have been affiliated as an adult volunteer with the Boy Scouts of America, happily serving youth and adopting the Scout Law as an important part of my ethical being. Of the twelve points of that law, none state "A Scout is truthful" because there is a greater law in Scouting: "A Scout is TRUSTWORTHY." And that is the bottom line for all of us in business. We should strive to be TRUSTWORTHY in our actions and deeds. People can depend on us to be truthful and trusted. A simple lie, caught immediately or much later, belies that trust.

Can you tell little business lies? Sure. But should you?

No negative surprises! Be first to warn of shortfalls.

In past insights, we've explored data gathering and dashboards for tracking the most important information to manage your company. Every good executive has a set of critical data points that best alert him or her to the changes in the flow of business, which are most important to note and in many cases to curb a negative trend early in the game.

There is a truism you should internalize: Most big problems start off as small problems. We'll call this the "rule of excursions." Small deviations from the trend or norm if unchecked often become much larger over time. A missed cash discount by your accounting department probably means that cash flow is getting tighter. Are receivables collections slowing? If so, is it one critical customer or a trend? Is it time to focus more resources upon collections, credit research, or even time to "fire some customers" who continually break your rules or take up too much of your resources?

Whatever the problem, the person or board to whom you report does not want to hear about it after it has become a threat to the enterprise. If you are the head of sales and the pipeline is emptying or sales have slowed for any sustained period, the red flag must be raised, even if the focus is on you as a result and not upon the problem when the news is first delivered. And if you're the CEO, your board definitely does not want to hear that revenues are about to fall through the floor because bookings for the past two periods have been so far below forecast.

An alert does not have to be too detailed or too long. It should be sent to your superiors (and everyone has one or more) quickly, often with a short "and we are working on finding the cause and redoubling our efforts." That's like a promise to self as well as to those who need to hear. And of course, a promise not kept is an indication of a lack of understanding of the problem or of care for the solution.

I have been a board member several times when either the board discovers a surprise or management delivers the news too late. Neither are good recipes for CEO survival. Not long ago, the board of one of my companies sat through an extended meeting just eight months after receiving a significant eight figure VC cash injection, reviewing income statements, budgets, sales statistics, Internet customer trends, and more. We discussed these with management thoroughly for a total of four hours. Three weeks later, the Board received a communication from the CEO that the company had only weeks of cash left and immediately needed another round.

Can you guess the mood of the board members? Management must have had some or total knowledge that cash was critical. But not a word was said, nor a discussion of alternatives suggested by the CEO or CFO, both present throughout the meeting. Well, both the CEO and CFO are now gone, and the VCs reluctantly passed the hat well before the budgeted cash-out date. And the terms of the new round were ominous, reflecting the anger and obvious catbird seat control the VCs had with no competition for their investment and too little progress to show from their last round.

Bad things happen to good people. But good managers do their utmost to make sure there are no large surprises such as that one.

Following up: Make your surprises positive.

Lots of people do or will depend upon your leadership in driving growth, stability, and profitability. There will always be times when salespersons or associates provide you with projections for future sales that reflect their inherent optimism.

Whether you in turn report to a CEO, a board or just your bank, you must reconcile such projections against the commitment of resources that will drain short term cash in expectation of revenues. Hiring call center employees, building raw materials or finished goods inventory, making that decision to expand space, all are made as a result of pressures from the past or expectation of growth in the future.

So, you bake some amount of these projections into your own budget and forecast and make decisions based upon the result. Some of us who've had extensive experience in senior management have lived by a rule of the 50's. Fifty percent of the salesperson's forecast rolls into cutting 50% of the sales VP forecast, making 25% of the initial salesperson forecast the operating budget. In a smaller company, the tendency to believe the numbers originally projected is higher because there are fewer levels of management and therefore more danger of overstatement. And some are so good at forecasting that this entire issue seems to be of no value. I had that discussion recently with several CEOs. I left the room wondering if they truly acted upon forecasts without change.

Even if you believe future revenues to be a solid guarantee, it is prudent to discount the numbers by some percentage so that planning for expenses is more conservative. Everyone feels great when surprises are positive. We don't celebrate just making our plan, we expect it. Instead, we celebrate overachievement and all it represents. Bankers, the board, shareholders, employees all love to see success. Think of the public company announcements of earnings, you see them instantly compared to analyst's projections. The market punishes anything but a positive surprise most of the time, a reflection that this insight is a part of the culture of the public markets.

Why pressure yourself, endanger the business and lose credibility by risking missed forecasts? We are rarely rewarded for the accuracy of our forecasts, and always are dunned when there is a shortfall. Think like Apple, a company that historically has always exceeded its forecasts to the delight of all stakeholders and respect of investors. We can't all be Apple, but we can learn at least this lesson from that company.

What's in it for me? Think like your stakeholders.

If you want to best describe the motivation behind the action, think "What's in it for me"? Your employees, your shareholders, your customers, and your suppliers are all driven by this question. So why not put yourself in their shoes and develop your action plan and goals to help each of them to achieve theirs?

Employees want to be challenged, appreciated, and rewarded for good work. So create a plan for each that will accomplish these goals upon successful achievement of their tasks over time. Be bold enough to ask each during their periodic reviews to tell you what they want to achieve. Be a good manager by creating paths to achievement that reflect those ambitions and allow the employee to measure success in a meaningful way during the effort to progress.

Suppliers need you to be a good customer, to pay a reasonable price for goods or services, to pay your bills on time, and of course to reorder when the time comes. But suppliers also want to know what makes you productive and help you win at your game. Good suppliers want to create solutions to your needs and distance themselves from their competition. So meet with critical suppliers and challenge them to meet your needs, asking how they can help solve your problems. Both sides win when you take the effort to inform, challenge, and partner with suppliers.

Your customers want to be treated as special. Each would like to know that they are important, genuinely important, to your success. Many would gladly share their problems with you hoping that you could provide solutions that would benefit both parties.

Your board members would experience a special feeling of accomplishment if they, as a group, could help you solve a problem that is strategic to the success of the company.

But deep within each of these stakeholders is the question baked into our psyche: "What's in it for me"? You can unlock lots of energy, talent and effort from each of these stakeholders merely by thinking ahead and planning your approach in response to that simple question.

This way to the exit: thinking strategically
By Gerard Miller

Every investor wants to know about the company's ultimate exit opportunities, the potential return on investment, timing, and the CEO's exit strategy - even if they change over time. Sadly, but honestly, not every exit is the one that everybody wanted; sometimes a cramdown or salvage sale is the endgame, despite best intentions and many months of hard work. And IPOs are only rarely the holy grail. So the roadmap to exits can have several twists and turns -- and surprise endpoints.

Every board should discuss at least annually the landscape for exits, so that they and the CEO have a clear understanding of what scenarios they may be working toward – or seeking to avoid. Usually, these discussions are best conducted in executive session with the CEO.

But as we know, hope is not a strategy. If the best achievable exit is to accept defeat or disappointment and grab what value for investors that the company can salvage, the time to begin exit discussions is "as soon as possible" when the slope is obviously slipping downward. If your CEO is reluctant to give up the ghost, this path becomes especially difficult for the investor directors, who may need to conduct an executive session to seek an outside advisor or banker.

Conversely, a growing company that has proven its expansion potential -- with successful products and sales -- can often exit happily by way of a corporate acquisition, a private equity buy-out, or a public stock offering (IPO or SPAC). In such scenarios, an investment banker is often engaged, to help the board ensure that it accepts the best deal possible on behalf of the investors.

Acquisition by another company may come as a result of a strategic partnership in which the acquirer is already familiar to the board, as is often the case with companies whose product is sold through the strategic investor's sales network. Some acquisitions of products and IP can become subject to bidding wars. Both scenarios usually require the board to retain some independent analysis of optimal value, to minimize the risk of a challenge by an aggrieved investor who claims they "could have done better." That protection is important under the business judgment rule. Often an expert on an M&A consultant team is surprisingly able to perform this analysis to set expectations for the board and protect its members by providing a second opinion.

The public-company exit option is the one most investors dream of, but that path is rare and may not be the best of all worlds – especially if premature. Use care here, as IPO's may provide an ego-based salve for founders and even for board members, whether appropriate and timely or not.

One of my portfolio companies is a biochemical company that went the IPO route to scoop up additional capital from new public shareholders to finish its FDA trials, and management feathered their nests in the new options pool. The company's early investors were locked up (unable contractually to sell before the end of six or more months after the IPO) - as the stock price cratered in a down market, and our capital gains dissolved. Now we face the paradox that if the long-sought FDA approvals are ultimately achieved, a predatory tender offer from Big Pharma with a modest premium just large enough to buy out the voting control will put a lid on our ultimate returns. For all practical purposes, the earlier investors have now lost much of their upside if clinical trials succeed. In this case, with hindsight, senior management and the board jumped the gun.

The bottom line for investor-directors: make sure your board retains sufficient, objective expertise, and members ask probing questions of the candidate advisory firms before engagement. If they are pitching an IPO, be sure to ask how much they will stand to make from their efforts above what they would make in an M&A sale, and to compare the approximate costs to the company in the process.

About the author...

Dave Berkus has a proven track record in operations, venture investing and corporate board service, both public and private. As an entrepreneur, he has formed, managed and sold successful businesses in the entertainment and software arenas. As a private equity investor, he has obtained healthy returns from liquidity events in over twenty-five investments in early-stage ventures. As a corporate mentor and director, he was named *"Director of the Year"* for his directorship efforts with over 40 companies in the past decade.

Dave was the founder of **Computerized Lodging Systems Inc.**, **(CLS)**, which he guided as founder and CEO for over a decade that included two consecutive years on the *Inc.500* list of America's fastest growing companies, expansion to six foreign subsidiaries and twenty-nine foreign distributors, while capturing 16% of the world market for his enterprise products. Known as a hospitality industry visionary with many "firsts" to his credit and for his accomplishments in advancing technology in the hospitality industry, in 1998 he was inducted into the **Hospitality (HFTP) "International Hall of Fame,"** one of only thirty so honored worldwide over the years.

He has made over 200 investments in early-stage ventures, for which he has an IRR of 97%, which includes capital contributions to his funds (**Berkus Technology Ventures, three Tech Coast Angels ACE funds -which Dave manages,** and **Kodiak Ventures, L.P.**, for which he was the managing partner before full payout.) He is also Chairman Emeritus of the Tech Coast Angels, one of the largest angel networks in the United States.

In recognition for adding significant shareholder value for emerging technology companies over the past decade, he was named

"Director of the Year-Early-Stage Businesses" by the *Forum for Corporate Directors* of Orange County, California and *"Technology Leader of the Year"* by the Los Angeles County Board of Supervisors. Dave currently sits on ten corporate boards and four non-profit boards.

Dave is also a senior partner in the twenty-year-old consulting firm of *Hospitality Automation Consultants, LTD (HACL)*, and lends his considerable visionary and strategic talents to worldwide hospitality chains and groups. He is the partner responsible for business process reorganization, strategic planning, software development and wide-area network infrastructure, and enterprise management systems.

A graduate of Occidental College, Dave currently serves as a Trustee of the College. Aside from this book, he is author of fourteen other books, twelve in the **BERKONOMICS** series, **GET SCRAPPY** as co-author, *"Extending the Runway"* originally published by Aspatore Press (and now by the BERKUS Press), and co-author of *"Better than Money!"* All are books for emerging growth technology company executives. Dave serves as Board Member of the San Gabriel Valley Council of *Boy Scouts of America*, former Board Member of the *Forum for Corporate Directors*, and is Chairman of the Advisory Board of the technology arm of the *ABL Organization*, a networking organization of CEOs in high tech businesses.

He is often engaged as keynote speaker for events worldwide, speaking on trends in technology and of legal and practical issues of governance for emerging company corporate boards. He tells stories of entrepreneurs who have wildly succeeded or failed, deriving lessons from each for his audience. His TEDx talk, *"Smile at success; Laugh at failure,"* is available on YouTube as are other segments of his keynotes. His weekly blog, "BERKONOMICS, is distributed to over 120,000 each week.

To contact Mr. Berkus for speaking engagements or workshops, email dberkus@berkus.com , or phone (626)355-5375. Dave's books are available for purchase from his personal Amazon bookstore under "Dave Berkus."

About the author...

Subscribe to the free weekly email or blog, www.Berkonomics.com, containing much of the information from Dave's books with lots of comments from readers with their own stories to tell.

Follow Dave on Twitter (@daveberkus) and LinkedIn (Dave Berkus).

Other books by Dave Berkus available directly from www.berkus.com or from your favorite bookseller or online store:

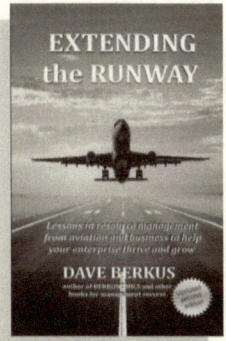

EXTENDING THE RUNWAY
Hard cover, soft cover, Kindle and Audible editions

The five tools board members and executives can use to help their companies succeed. How boards and CEOs should relate to each other for growing the enterprise. Fifty-eight critical questions boards and management should consider in order to assure their mutual alignment.

BASIC BERKONOMICS
Hard cover, soft cover and eBook editions

Volume one of this series. Over one hundred critical insights for entrepreneurs, CEOs and board members covering the life of the company from ignition through liquidity event. Written with basic explanations for terms and methods, as well as insights into planning and measurement for success with small business startups.

BERKONOMICS
Hard cover, soft cover, Kindle and Audible editions

Volume two of this series. One hundred and one critical insights for entrepreneurs, CEOs and board members covering the life of the company from ignition through liquidity event. Dave tells over fifty stories to illustrate his insights, culled from his experience as an entrepreneur and service on over forty corporate and ten non-profit boards.

BERKONOMICS WORKBOOK
Companion to BERKONOMICS, this very personal journal contains 101 exercises for the CEO or manager that make each of the insights contained in BERKONOMICS come to life in the form of provocative and actionable questions to be answered right on the pages of the workbook. Once completed, this workbook becomes the manager's personal blueprint for business growth.

ADVANCED BERKONOMICS

Hard cover, soft cover and eBook editions

Volume two of this series. One hundred and one critical insights for entrepreneurs, CEOs and board members covering the life of the company from ignition through liquidity event.   More advanced insights into planning and measurement for success with small business startups.

GET SCRAPPY

Hard cover, soft cover and eBook editions

Co-authored with Kim Shepherd, this book continues the BERKONOMICS series with the addition of excellent contributions from a co-author highly experienced in team management, remote work, and corporate culture.

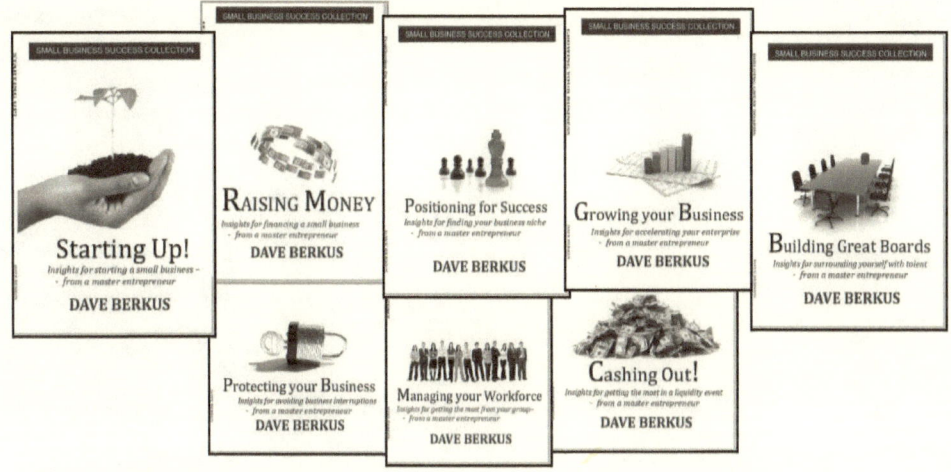

SMALL BUSINESS SUCCESS SERIES
A Series of eight short and inexpensive books or eBooks

Take all the great material in the BERKONOMICS series and slice it by subject, and you'll have these eight inexpensive, short books about issues that you and your management team needs to focus upon today. Ideal for giving to your entire management group for group discussions and business planning sessions.

BOOKS and eBOOKS IN THIS SERIES:

1. *Starting up!*
2. *Raising Money*
3. *Positioning for Success*
4. *Managing your Workforce*
5. *Protecting your Business*
6. *Growing your Business*
7. *Building Great Boards*
8. *Cashing Out!*

www.ingramcontent.com/pod-product-compliance
Lightning Source LLC
Chambersburg PA
CBHW030009190526
45157CB00014B/1822